STO

FRIENDS
OF ACPL

FOSSILS

FROM THIS EARTH

William Russell

The Rourke Corporation, Inc.
Vero Beach, Florida 32964

PHOTO CREDITS:
© James P. Rowan: cover and page 8;
© William Russell: title page, pages 4, 10, 12, 13, 15, 21;
courtesy of The Mammoth Site: pages 7 and 18;
courtesy John Day Fossil Beds National Monument: page 17

Library of Congress Cataloging-in-Publication Data

Russell, William, 1942–
  Fossils / by William Russell.
    p. cm. — (From this earth)
  Includes index
  ISBN 0-86593-358-8
  1. Fossils—Juvenile literature. [1. Fossils.]
I. Title II. Series.
QE714.5.R86 1994
560—dc20   94-2402
                                               CIP
                                               AC
Printed in the USA

TABLE OF CONTENTS

FOSSILS

No one has seen a dinosaur. But we know that dinosaurs once roamed the Earth. Like many other living things, the dinosaurs left something behind—fossils.

Fossils are the **ancient**, or very old, remains of plants and animals. Dinosaur remains are millions of years old. Other fossils are from living things that died much more recently—several thousand years ago.

KINDS OF FOSSILS

Most plant and animal remains rot away. Some, however, are **preserved**, or saved, in various ways by nature.

Animal fossils are often teeth, bones or shells. Rarely, even whole bodies of animals may be preserved. At other times, a fossil is no more than a print left by the plant or animal.

Over thousands or millions of years, some of the remains that become fossils **petrify**, or harden. Ancient trees that turned to stone are called petrified wood.

Woolly mammoth bones in rock at The Mammoth Site in Hot Springs, South Dakota

WHERE FOSSILS ARE FOUND

Fossils are plentiful. Nearly every part of North America, as well as other lands, has fossils.

Most fossils are found in rocks that were formed of mud and sand. Fossils have also been found in ice, tar and the ancient **sap** of trees.

Entire woolly **mammoths** have been found in the ice of Alaska and Siberia. Thousands of years ago, a few of these ancient elephants were quick-frozen by nature.

Thousands of years ago, the LaBrea Tar Pits in Los Angeles trapped animals and preserved their remains. (This imperial mammoth at LaBrea is a model.)

HOW FOSSILS ARE MADE

Nature has many ways to preserve plant and animal remains. **Minerals** play a part in the making of many fossils.

Minerals are the solid substances which make up the Earth's crust. Certain minerals found in water may soak into dead plants and animals. Over long periods, the minerals harden parts of the animal or plant.

Minerals hardened and changed the color of this tooth from a huge shark which died thousands of years ago

*Petrified wood—wood turned to stone—lies in
Petrified Forest National Park, Arizona*

Ancient shell fossils in limestone rock

FINDING FOSSILS

Many fossils are buried in mud or rock. But as rocks and earth are worn away, fossils are revealed. Ocean currents and fast-moving floodwater, for example, wash away soil and loose rock. Moving water uncovers great numbers of fossils. At some beaches, fossils wash ashore by the thousands.

Fossils may be uncovered by highway, home and canal building. **Weathering**—the wearing away of rock and soil from rain and other weather conditions—also reveals fossils.

Ancient sharks teeth and other animal fossils are plentiful along some seashores

THE FOSSIL "BOOK"

Fossils are a book, a record, of life on Earth. The fossil book is not perfect. Many kinds of plants and animals lived and died without leaving fossils. And most fossils will never be found.

The fossils that are found, however, tell us many things about the plants and animals that once lived on Earth. The location of fossils in the ground helps explain much about ancient Earth.

Fossils help scientists and artists understand how ancient plants and animals looked and lived

STUDYING FOSSILS

Fossil scientists know that what is today a dry grassland may have been an ancient jungle. Mountains rise today where an ancient sea was.

Scientists learn such things by studying the fossils of a region.

Scientists believe they can measure the age of most fossils. The scientists use a process called radiocarbon dating.

FOSSILS ON NATIONAL LANDS

One of America's greatest fossil "books" is the Grand Canyon in Arizona. The flow of the Colorado River cuts steep canyon walls up to a mile deep in the rock.

Fossils in these walls tell scientists much about life on Earth millions of years ago. The oldest fossils are those closest to the bottom of the canyon.

The Grand Canyon is one of several public lands where fossils are protected for everyone to see, enjoy and study.

The mile-deep Grand Canyon in Grand Canyon National Park is a treasure chest of fossils

PETRIFIED FOREST NATIONAL PARK

Petrified Forest National Park in Arizona is an amazing place. It is a forest of fallen stone trees! For miles, the ground is heaped with pieces of colorful, petrified wood. Some of the stone logs are 125 feet long and 225,000,000 years old.

Among the other national parks and monuments rich with fossils are Florissant Fossil Beds and Dinosaur in Colorado. Badlands in South Dakota and John Day Fossil Beds in Oregon are also great places to see and learn about fossils in North America.

Glossary

ancient (AIN chent) — very old

mammoth (MAH muth) — a type of ancient elephant that lived in North America and disappeared thousands of years ago

mineral (MIN er uhl) — any of several natural, non-living materials which occur in the Earth

petrify (PEH truh fi) — to change into stone over long periods of time

preserve (pre ZERV) — to save in a protected place

sap (SAP) — a liquid in trees and other plants

weathering (WEH thur ing) — the wearing away of rock and soil by rain and other weather conditions

INDEX